GREETINGS FOR

CHRISTMAS

AND A HAPPY

NEW YEAR

Seeing Stars

by
Harold Kohn

1908 Grand Avenue
Nashville, Tennessee 37203

Library of Congress Catalog Number: 71-182396
© 1971 by TIDINGS, 1908 Grand Avenue, Nashville,Tenn. 37203
S336B

To
LAWRENCE AND MILDRED TENHOPEN,
our successors in the Gospel ministry,
cherished friends,
and
faithful servants of Christ

Introduction

Smog shrouded cities, dying rivers, and mountains washing to the sea have awakened in us a new sense of concern about life on this planet.

Until recently, there were only a few persons who had this concern. Few who could see in nature the handiwork of God and realize how intimately all of life is tied to every other living thing. Dr. Harold Kohn has been one of those few prophetic spokesmen who not only speaks about, but consistently works at restoring the natural order.

Dr. Kohn has the ability to see the beauty, mystery, and wonder of nature. His illustrations show his intimate knowledge of the natural order. Because of this intense interest and broad knowledge every drawing and illustration speaks with the authentic ring of truth.

More significantly, Dr. Kohn sees beyond the beauty of the natural order.

For him creation is a textbook telling of the Creator; or perhaps more like a personal letter from the Creator to all mankind. A letter that speaks of order, planning, consistency, trustworthiness, and care. Harold Kohn opens the readers' eyes to the truth of God revealed in creation.

Seeing Stars is written for everyone. The style and manner of writing and illustration major on simplicity. Simplicity like that of a flower, whose fragrance and beauty are easily comprehended and enjoyed by curious child or learned adult. Dr. Kohn writes for every man.

It is a pleasure to welcome you to the growing list of those who find Dr. Harold Kohn's writing about the creation a new revelation of the Creator.

Rueben P. Job
EDITOR

Contents

Thanks for the Glad Season

O God, Eternal Father, how glad we are to be alive at Christmastime! Glad to see the starlight; glad for snowfall; glad for loved ones near; glad for laughter ringing through our rooms and happy greetings shouted in the streets; glad for Christmas carols; glad for Christmas messages found in daily mail, in books, in pulpits; glad for the wonder and excitement of little children; glad for countless deeds of kindness and love.

We are gladdened, above all else, by memories of the old, ever-new story of thy coming among us in a Baby's small form, the everlasting Truth, the unspeakable Beauty, the unfathomable Goodness "wrapped in swaddling clothes, lying in a manger."

Gladden others around us, our Father, through the contagious joy that Christ has given us. Thus may the miracle of Christmas spread around the world. Through Christ our Lord. Amen.

Seeing Stars

Only in the darkness do we see the stars; and when the night is darkest, stars shine most brightly.

It was the darkness of their times that made it possible for wise men to follow the star to the manger of Bethlehem where they found Christ.

Wise men of every age learn how to use darkness to find the Light, and the gloomiest times to find God.

How Big Is the Baby?

On birth announcements the name of the baby, its sex, the name of the parents, the date and place of birth are written, and then near the bottom of the announcement the weight and length of the baby are given. Everyone wants to know, "How big is the baby?"

At Christmastime when we celebrate the birth of history's most important child, one natural question to ask is, "How big is the Baby?" Is he a premature infant, coming before his time into a world too much for him? Is he strong enough? Can he survive?

He was bigger than his people's conception of the Messiah.

He was bigger than the hard, rigid rules of his people; bigger than their legalisms or ours.

He is bigger than the churches of the Church, bigger than the theologies that have grown up around him.

His cross was tall, but he stands taller. He is bigger than death and the tomb.

Joseph

While he was God reduced to man-size, flesh of our flesh, he was too big to be crowded into the term "man"; there was too much of him for that.

None of our ways are sufficient for him. He is the Way that is greater than our ways. None of our truths quite describe or cover him. He is the Truth too big for our lesser truths. None of earth's lights equal him or dim his splendor: he is the Light from which our lesser lights borrow their flame.

He seems too big to comprehend even now, after the passage of all these centuries. The churches and their scholars and theologians still differ in their interpretations of him, just as people who see different sides of the same mountain differ in descriptions of it.

How big is the Baby of Bethlehem? No one yet has taken his measure. His meaning eludes all human measurements. But he is healthy. Long after Caesar, Herod, Rome, and all his enemies are gone, he will survive.

17

Unclutter

One lesson on Christmas is that we must learn to unclutter our lives if we are to be attentive to God. And this does not mean merely junking the evil; it means putting aside the good that keeps us from the best. Shepherds left their flocks—their work which materially sustained them—to visit the Babe in the manger. And wise men did not let other stars distract them from that heavenly light that led them to Bethlehem and the Savior.

Comparatively few people are kept from Christ by some great, towering evil standing in their way. Most do not bow before the "best" God has given us because they are already preoccupied with good things, their busy work, acquiring wealth, enjoying entertainments, pleasures and comforts. So the "best" life is missed while tending to the "good" life. Sheep-tending is a great good, but those shepherds who found Christ that first Christmas had to leave it for awhile to seek the Savior.

Lesser lights must often be ignored, wise men know, if we are to see the Eternal Light.

Drenched With the Christmas Faith

Our Father, let us never become discouraged by thy small and weak beginnings, now that we see what thou didst begin with the Baby of Bethlehem.

Preserve us from despondency when we are tempted to be dejected by the terrible power of evil. By the splendid recollection that it is the Christ child's birthday we now celebrate, and not Caesar's or Herod's, may we take new hope and trust that, while evil has its moment, thou dost own the ages. In ways we can but faintly guess, thy will prevails at last.

Let all our days become gloriously drenched with this Christmas faith. In Christ's name. Amen.

Peace

How We Spend Christmas

We do not know how much the wise men paid for their gifts of gold, frankincense, and myrrh, or which wise man spent the most for his present, or how much effort and time were invested by shepherds in leaving their flocks to visit the manger in Bethlehem.

One thing the wise men and shepherds had in common: they all came to the cattle stall to worship the newly born King.

Now, as then, *how* we spend Christmas is much more important than *how much* we spend for Christmas.

The Greatest Poverty—
The Greatest Wealth

The greatest poverty in the world is unawareness. There are no glories for the inattentive, no wonders for the indifferent. There is no Bethlehem star for those who persist in the downward look and no angel voices proclaiming the Savior's birth for those who listen only to the noisy clamor of earth.

The poorest person in Bethlehem that first Christmas night was the prosperous innkeeper who provided no room in his inn for Joseph and Mary and for the Baby about to be born. He afforded them no room in the inn because he was unaware of the glory coming to Bethlehem. A crowded inn meant unusual profits for the innkeeper, but he remained poor nevertheless. While he had a full cash bag he had an empty soul.

The rich are not those who fill their pocket books,

strong boxes, safes, and stock portfolios with worldly wealth. The world's wealthy are those who fill their minds with truth and their souls with beauty and goodness.

The richest people on earth that first Christmas night were poor shepherds and dear, modest Mary and Joseph, who owned little. The Baby owned them.

The Innkeeper

Christ on Our Shopping List

Forgive us, our Father, when we have bestowed gifts on all our loved ones at Christmas, but have forgotten him whose birthday we celebrate. Show us some way to put Christ on our shopping list. While we may find no suitable present for him in the merchandise heaped in the stores, surely his cause needs our time, our energy, our money.

Make us now more alert than ever to those human needs with which our Lord identified himself, the needs of the ill-fed and poorly clothed, the lonely, the sad, and the outcasts.

Though we err foolishly in other ways, our Father, grant us a genius for giving the needed gift at the appropriate time where it will do the most good, and to those who can in no way repay us. Thus may we celebrate Christmas all year long in the spirit of the One who is thy gift to humankind. Amen.

The Fearless Heart

The fearless heart depends upon a vivid sense of God's presence.

Read again the first Christmas story of how terror turned to wonder, joy, and adoration as the shepherds became aware of the God who came among them in the person of "the babe lying in a manger."

Saint Luke's Gospel informs us, "And there were in the same country shepherds abiding in the field, keeping watch over their flock by night. And, lo, the angel of the Lord came upon them, and the glory of the Lord shone round about them; and they were sore afraid. And the angel said unto them, 'Fear not: for, behold, I bring you good tidings of great joy, which shall be to all people. For unto you is born this day in the city of David a Savior, which is Christ the Lord.'

"And it came to pass, as the angels were gone away from them into heaven, the shepherds said one to another, 'Let us now go even unto Bethlehem, and see this thing which is come to pass, which the Lord hath made known unto us.' And they came with haste, and found Mary and Joseph, and the babe lying in a manger. And when they had seen it, they made known abroad the saying which was told them concerning this child. And all they that heard it wondered at those things which were told them by the shepherds." (Luke 2:8-11;15-18)

Fear is usually a self-centered emotion, a heightened awareness of danger to either our own physical welfare or our own ego-interests. To the self-centered every rustle is terrifying, even the brush of angel wings, and every voice is threatening, even an angel's song. The best cure for fear is in the replacement of excessive self-consciousness with a consciousness of others and their needs, or, above all, the awareness of Another, infinitely greater than all others, who is lovingly near us.

Sound religion is mostly a life-controlling awareness of God's presence.

Repeat the Joy

The entire realm of creation demonstrates the need for repetition of vital processes.

No matter how healthy and full may be the first breath a baby draws, the first gasp of air will be insufficient to supply the infant with oxygen for the remainder of his life. The child must repeatedly take more breaths as long as he survives. Failure to repeat means death. So with heartbeats, eating, and sleeping. Thus it is, also, with sunrises and sunsets, the coming and going of seasons, and the countless processes which make life here possible and beautiful: repetition lies at the heart of existence.

Jesus frequently spoke of himself in figures signifying the sustained, continuing relationship his disciples were to have with him. Bread, water, light, and physician were some of the likenesses he drew, picturing himself in relationship to his followers. These things we need repeatedly. Taking care of them today will not suffice for tomorrow. The need returns repeatedly, and the answer to the need must be repeatedly available. So with the truths of Christmas. We need a fresh, daily look at the God whom Christ revealed.

One of our favorite Christmas carols is "Joy to the World! The Lord Is Come." The second stanza of the carol is sung, "Joy to the world! The Saviour reigns: Let men their songs employ; While fields and floods, rocks, hills and plains Repeat the sounding joy, Repeat the sounding joy, Repeat, repeat the sounding joy." There is solid truth in these phrases. The great glad gospel was not meant merely to be proclaimed, but to be repeated. Like breaths, heartbeats, eating and sleeping, like prayer and sacrificial self-giving, the good news that the Creator of the universe is Christlike—patient, loving, merciful, forgiving, and redemptive, and as near to us as our own flesh—is necessarily and gloriously repetitive. It is the glad word that, when repeated daily, sustains our souls.

The central message of Christmas is either relevant to all seasons, or it is irrelevant to every season. The gospel of Christmas is either meaningful to everyday life, or it is meaningless on Christmas Day. It is worthy of frequent repetition or it is unworthy of a first telling.

Christmas is not a story to be told once, or an experience to be lived once, but a joyful gospel that is as fitting to the twenty-sixth of December as to the twenty-fifth, and as meaningful in July as in December.

32

Our pioneer forefathers made candles by dipping bits of string repeatedly into a vat of melted tallow or wax until several layers of the light-giving substance were added to the cord.

In a similar way the devout soul dips his mind again and again into the most strengthening, hopeful, trust-bestowing ideas he knows, so that his thought-life can shine brightly, and his entire life be illumined. The best idea of all is God's Big Idea, the Word made flesh, the one truth we most need to know: the God of the Universe is Christ-like.

33

No Falling Star

May a stumbling, lost, wandering world now get its bearings from Bethlehem.

We have been misled by the lure of bigness, by the power of temporal might and by the glamour of success and worldly wealth. Let this confused generation reset its course and find its way across the wastes of narrow self-interest, materialism, hatred, and warfare to thy living forgiveness and peace.

At Bethlehem, where Christ's infant voice was first heard on the thin night air, may we find where we are, who we are, to whom we belong, and how thou wouldst have us live.

Let not the light above Bethlehem become a falling star, a flashing brilliance soon gone out of sight, out of mind.

Rather, may thy guiding Light stay central in our vision. Like the wise men, may we follow it on our earthly journey until we come at last to the ultimate reverence, bowing in unreserved devotion and complete commitment wherever we find thee, through Christ. Amen.

When You Wish Upon a Star

At only one time of the year would you dream of cutting an evergreen tree and planting it in your living room. In only one season of the year would you hang your family's stockings from the fireplace mantle, or in some other conspicuous spot in your house, and leave them there as appropriate decorations and receptacles for gifts. At no other time would you practice the extravagant generosity that typifies the behavior of most of us in December. Christmastime is characterized by strange human behavior.

Strangeness marked the first Christmas, too. Consider these odd events that still hold the wonder of the world: the Infant King born in a cattle stall rather than in a palace bedroom; Herod's fear of the Baby; humble shepherds chosen to hear angel voices telling of Christ's coming, while sophisticates went about their duties and pleasures, unaware of the glory that had come among them: Wise Men from the east, longing for the coming of a Savior, following a star's light on a long, hazardous, wearisome journey to Bethlehem to find the newly born Redeemer.

Many of the world's children make a wish upon the first star they see in the heavens when darkness falls. The Wise Men with beautiful childlike faith wished upon a star, and it led them to Christ. How strange, how gloriously, unforgettably strange those Wise Men were!

The Realistic Wish

Could the Wise Men be charged with "wishful thinking"? Perhaps. The Wise Men *were* wishful. But theirs was not an unrealistic wish. They were not afflicted by some foolish optimism that "Believing will make it so." Nor is there any indication that they held the common view, hardly a devout one, that "*Somehow* things will change for the better," or "Everything will turn out all right, if given enough time."

The Wise Men saw man's situation realistically. The world was sinful, and the world did need a Savior. It was time

for the Redeemer to come. Their own role in this event was to watch for a sign—a certain star—to follow the star until they came to the Savior, and to give Him their unreserved devotion.

Wishful Thinking at Its Worst and Best

Wishful thinking is harmful when it is used for purposes of self-deception, when it is an evasion of facts we do not dare face, when it becomes a habit of daydreaming where there is urgent work to be done. At its worst wishful thinking is a fleeing from the facts of a situation.

At its best, wishful thinking alters a situation for the better. Before we can clean up our polluted human environment, we must wish for more nearly sanitary, uncontaminated surroundings.

Before we can rid the world of war we must have a fervent desire to give up national greed, to redirect national pride. Man must learn to disagree non-violently, to reach out with helping hand to each other rather than to shake clenched fists, to fight against war itself as the worst enemy of nations.

Such wishful thinking is no timid flight from reality. It makes tussling with stern realities possible. Wishing one could do something to prevent life-destroying disease and ease the world's pain does not make the practice of medicine or surgery unreal. A young person must first have that desire before he can become a worthy doctor.

Wishing a certain beloved person could be one's

partner for life, does not make a marriage unreal. It makes marriage compelling.

Wishing for a baby does not make a pregnancy or a birth unreal. The deeply desired baby is as real, and far more fortunate, than the unwished for child.

Wishing upon a star, did not make the far journey from the east unreal to the Wise Men that first Christmas. Rather, wishing made it possible and urgent. Only by wishing for the Savior's coming and then putting their eager yearning into action did the Wise Men find Christ. They did not flee from the facts of life but hastened toward the Central Fact of human history, the Child in the manger bed.

Season of Good Wishes

It is the business of Christmas to play carols of hope upon our wishes. It is the season of good wishes, ranging all the way from "I wish you a Merry Christmas" to wishing we were much wiser; wishing we were more worthy husbands and wives, children or parents; wishing we were better ministers or laymen, employees or employers; wishing we could make tithes and offerings stretch to cover more causes; wishing Christ's kingdom were really realized in international relations, in our community, in our place of work, in our churches and homes; wishing we were better Christians.

Wishes That Are Strong Enough

The present state of the world is discouraging to any

thinking person and simply wishing the world were better will not improve it. But unless a person has a desire for a better world, there is no moral imperative to improve it.

Sanctified wishful thinking at its best rests upon faith that there are possibilities for redeeming the world, that the Redeemer has a chance on earth in spite of Caesar and Herod, in spite of the indifference of much of humankind and the hostility of many, in spite of a cross and a tomb.

Wise Men of the first Christmas and of every age do not believe that God has futilely exhausted his love for mankind or his power to save men from sin's destruction. They long for God's further action, for a sure sign God cares. Their desire for salvation is not weak or luke-warm, but strong enough to gather up their fragmented thoughts and loves into a mighty effort to become acquainted with the Redeemer and to introduce Him to the world.

Wishes Converted into Deeds

Moreover, the Wise Men *acted* in terms of their desire. They did not remain comfortably at home in the east with their wishes. Instead, they travelled the long, arduous, star-lit path to Bethlehem. When they stopped at Herod's palace and Herod asked them to return and let him know where the child could be found, they protected the Baby from Herod's schemes to take His life.

When the Wise Men saw the baby they responded appropriately, giving the Highest their highest homage and bestowing upon Him gifts that would bespeak their adoration long after they had left Bethlehem. In short, the Wise Men's good wishes were converted into good deeds. The desire for the Savior's coming mobilized their thoughts, plans and actions so that loving concern became loving deeds.

The Wisdom of Wishing Upon a Star

Isn't this one of the chief weaknesses of religion in our time, that it has largely lost its capacity for a worthy wishfulness, a fervent desire with glad expectation in it? There must be a hole in our faith through which we have lost the wondrous belief that God has something astonishingly good in store for us.

We do not expect enough of God, or the right things. We live frantically, strenuously and plagued by discouragement, as if we had no strength other than our own to draw upon. The chaos and misery of the world embitters us. The world has become cynical about man, and man's power to set things right.

It is at just such a time that we need the wisdom of Wise Men who believed God would do what man by his own strength could not do, who had given up godless self-sufficiency for hope in the coming Savior, who wished upon a star and followed its light until they found Christ.

41

Christmas Says It Is So

In a world Created and sustained by the God Christ has revealed we dare to be wishful thinkers and wishful believers.

Wouldn't it be wonderful if Infant Goodness were stronger than grown evil and the Baby Jesus were potentially more powerful than Caesar? Christmas says it is so. It is Christ's birthday we now celebrate, not Caesar's. The indifferent and devout alike date their documents and letters *A.D.*, 1970 anno Domini, "the year of our Lord," for history is registered in Christ's name, not Caesar's.

Wouldn't it be wonderful if God were in control of things, rather than evil forces always having their way with the world? Christmas says it is so. God is in control, ultimately. Caesar and Herod have their moments, but Christ has His centuries, His millennia, His Eternity. Evil has to rush about, accomplishing its fleeting purposes in a wicked frenzy of haste, for God and time are faithful allies.

Wouldn't it be wonderful if the glory of God were not reserved for king's palaces, but could be found amidst commonplace things and ordinary people such as ourselves, as well? Christmas says it is so. Remember that austerely simple cattle stall, and the shepherd folk, and the peasant mother and carpenter Joseph, and the One who was found there among them.

Wouldn't it be wonderful if the original Christmas

story could withstand the ravages of time, the erosion of retelling and the rust of familiarity and come to us in our generation of crucial need unbroken and unbreakable? Of course, the joy-filled story of Christmas has done just that.

Wouldn't it be wonderful if Christmas were not tethered to that first Christmas Day? What a splendid thing, if Christmas could spread throughout all time from Bethlehem to every town, from the manger to every home, from the hearts of Joseph, Mary and the Baby to human hearts the world around. It can happen. This Christmas it will be so.

Wouldn't it be wonderful if at least once each year much of mankind would take the time to thrust aside every trifle, especially life's little annoyances, to forget self in the interest of others, to look at one another with loving appreciation and gratitude, to become more interested in giving than in getting, to try to plumb the significance of that heartbreakingly beautiful Event of long ago Bethlehem, and to let its meaning overflow into the here and now, saturating all our days? It can happen. It does happen. Christmas makes it so.

Too Good to Be True?

If anything were too good to be true, Christmas would be. But if Christmas is not too good to be true, nothing can be.

Dare to wish fervently and to entertain great expectations, for in a world where God reduces Himself to

43

Infant size to make Himself known to us, anything astonishingly good can happen.

Christmas says it is so.

Light Upon Our Pathway

We thank Thee, O Thou Eternal Spirit, for ways in which our lives today are enriched by influences from the past that touch the present moment with splendor. For the words of ancient prophets, wise men, poets and heroes that come to us from Thy Holy Word and from human history we praise Thee.

For memories of the goodness of parents, brothers and sisters, friends and neighbors, teachers and counsellors, we are grateful, for from them a tender light falls upon our pathway illumining the next steps we must take.

Keep us ever aware, O God, that as surely as our lives bear the imprint of other lives, so we cannot avoid influencing those around us. Enrich us with Thy grace and empower us with Thy Spirit so that when we impart portions of ourselves to others they may be refreshed and strengthened. May we light warm fires in cold rooms.

Grant us this further gift, our Father, the power to do much Christlike good in the world without our knowing it.

In the name of Christ, our Lord. Amen.

A Test of True Wisdom

The "realists" are right at one point: we dare not use religion to escape facing life's ugly facts, to ignore what we hate to see.

It is often true, as the ancient proverb puts it, that "a man gazing at the stars is at the mercy of the puddles on the road." But our most tragic mistake is not that of blundering into puddles. Our error is greater and sadder: we are so preoccupied with mud puddles that we fail to see the stars.

The Wise Men of the East were not so absorbed in earthly things that they missed the star of Bethlehem.

Perhaps this is a test of true wisdom—the capacity to see life whole, to blend tough realism with tender idealism: to let both the earthly and the heavenly have our attention, to develop keen eyesight that detects mud puddles and deep insight that measures the significance of the new light that God sheds upon our way, to recognize Herod, while seeking the Holy Child.

Herod

The Language of Kindness

O Lord, help me to learn well the language of kindness, which even the slow of mind can understand, the deaf can hear and the blind can read. Amen.

Happiness and Joy

Happiness is less a goal already achieved than a worthy destination eagerly sought and travelled toward with single-minded abandon. And mere happiness becomes great joy when the goal is the known will of God and Christ is the Companion along the way.

First Day and Last Day

Eternal God, my Father, help me to live today in joyous wonder and gratitude, as if it were the first day I had ever seen. And may I live this day responsibly, intensely and meaningfully, as if it were my last day on earth. Amen.

A Sense of the Sacred

When psychologist William Moulton Marston asked three thousand persons, "What have you to live for?" he was dumb-founded to discover that ninety-four percent were merely enduring today while awaiting some imagined happiness in a far-off tomorrow. Some were longing for freedom from responsibility they expected to find when their children grew up and left home. A number looked forward to a trip they had dreamed of for years. A few were anticipating an inheritance which would make life easier. While they had big ambitions for the tomorrows, they evidently did not have much appetite for today, for savouring today's meals, rejoicing in today's sunshine, excited by today's small adventures, resting in tonight's sleep.

A God Who Is Somewhere Else

A similar fault mars the lives of many "religious"

people. They believe in a God, but in a God who is usually somewhere else. When they are at work, God is at church. But when they are in church, God is in heaven. Or he is present in such sacraments as baptism and marriage rituals which occur only occasionally, but they do not sense His presence while reading biography or the newspaper, in family conversation, or in laughter.

Or they feel if they could only spend more time by a lonely lakeshore they might "find God in nature," but they have no awareness of His nearness on the elevated commuter train, in the subway, in the factory, the office or the ghetto.

But God is not confined to churches which men have constructed. Even the Bible teaches that temples made by human hands cannot contain all of God. Nor is God imprisoned in heaven. The whole universe is His sanctuary. Wherever and whenever our minds and hearts are hospitable to God, He answers our invitation to companionship. The Psalmist, who celebrated his faith in the temple, also found the Lord "in green pastures," "beside still waters," in "the valley of the shadow of death" and "in the presence of mine enemies." In harmony with the Psalmist's view, William Cowper expressed his conviction of the sanctity of all places where there is a divine-human encounter, singing:

> "Jesus, where'er thy people meet,
> There they behold thy mercy seat.
> Where'er they seek thee,

> thou art found
> And every place is holy ground."

What Is a Sacrament?

In the history of the Christian Church special events and symbols were given recognition as "Sacraments," or "Sacred things" because they were hallowed by their association with the Divine. These were visible signs that fixed man's wandering thoughts on the ever-present God whom we often miss, partly because He is always near.

The traditions of Roman Catholicism support seven sacraments—baptism, confirmation, penance, the holy eucharist, extreme unction, holy orders and matrimony. Most Protestants observe only two sacraments—baptism and the Lord's supper, while the Friends (known also as Quakers) observe no particular rite as peculiarly sacramental, because they claim all of life should be regarded as sacred. All sacraments are outward, physical signs of inner, spiritual realities. They are means of making us conscious of the God who is always in our midst, but whose presence is frequently forgotten or overlooked.

But to the deeply sensitive soul, pervaded by God-consciousness, everything on earth is a sacrament since it reminds him of the Eternal and nourishes his faith. (Even an observed sinful act prompts him to remember the soul's weakness when it does not rely on God.)

Worship, Work and Fellowship

Worship is sacramental when we are paying attention to God, as well as asking Him to be attentive to our needs; when the soul is bowed in reverence, adoration and wholehearted commitment to the known will of God, and in search of more knowledge of that will; when ritual and symbols are not ends in themselves, but prompters that recall to us our high origin and destiny and Him who is the Way.

But work, as well as worship, is a sacrament when it is performed with a sense of vocation or "calling" by God to daily tasks.

Fellowship is sacred, for it is a bond that reminds us that our influence depresses or elevates those around us, dragging them closer to hell or lifting them nearer to heaven.

Eating, Sleeping and Awakening

Partaking of meals is a holy act, for the devout person recognizes that many unseen people from places near and far away have labored that he might be fed, and all of the labor would have been in vain if it were not for merciful rains, the beneficent sun, and the Heavenly Father's will.

Sleep is sacramental when it means trustfully giving up the reins of life because we know God is in control. And awakening is a sacrament when it is arousal to duties we deem worthy of a child of God.

Birth, Death, Success and Failure

The birth of a child is sacred, for it hints of God's hope for humanity. It is a new, fresh beginning. And the death of any of God's children is sacramental when it calls to mind that we are but transients here, travelling toward our Father's House, and the good we intend to do must be done quickly.

Success is sacramental if it reminds us of all who have aided us on our way, especially that Helper without whom all human effort is in vain. Failure is sacramental, too, when it reminds us that human nature is flawed, and thus frees us of our vanity, when it affords opportunity to learn from a mistake and start over, and when it compels us to trust in Him who redeems our lives from destruction.

Sickness as Sacramental

If one has a sense of the sacred, even suffering can be converted into a sacrament. It, too, is a physical situation which serves the spiritually sensitive person as an outward, visible sign of an inward, physical grace.

A well-used serious illness shakes our foolish confidence in our own strength, upsets our unrealistic self-sufficiency and unsettles our false securities. It shatters our tendency to take tomorrow for granted. (Although, too often we return to this proneness once the illness is past.) Sickness teaches trust in those things that germs and viruses cannot invade, physical infirmity cannot weaken and accident cannot maim.

In suffering those who seek the Great Physician learn who He is, how He loves, and what He can do, as did the sick at Capernaum, the blind, deaf, lame, leprous and insane of many a Palestinean town and countryside, and as did a pain-ridden thief by His side on the cross. Those who use sickness sacramentally become better because of the body's distress.

"Holy as a Church"

Florence Nightingale illustrates the meaning of sacramental living. In reference to Miss Nightingale, "the lady with the lamp" and the inspiration of modern nursing, a soldier wrote from the hospital at Scutari, "What a comfort it was to see her even pass. She would speak to one and nod and smile to as many more; but she could not do it to all, you know. We lay there by hundreds: but we could kiss her shadow as it fell and lay our heads on the pillow again content." Another said of her, "Before she came there was cursing and swearing, but after that it was holy as a church."

In a day when female nurses were barely tolerated by the medical profession, Florence Nightingale served the sick and wounded, clamping her jaws tightly shut while nerving herself to help with operations where anesthetics were not used, penning final messages to the sweethearts, wives and mothers of mortally wounded soldiers, quoting verses of Scripture or murmuring a stanza of a favorite hymn to a depressed soldier, until the military hospital became a holy place and her every act a sacra-

61

ment. Her visible acts of kindness were clear reminders of the invisible mercy of God.

Living the sacramental life means placing all of our existence under the control of our consciousness of God, until the most unlikely situations become filled with His glory. And sacramental living means a style of life of such quality that what we do and are reminds others of the nearness and goodness of God.

He Disturbs Our Peace

One truth the "peace of mind" cults have never been able to face is that Jesus, whom they like to think of as "the gentle Galilean," was not always gentle in his treatment of the traditions of His people, or in His dealings with the leaders of His faith or the church of His time. He often caused people trouble.

Jesus and Religious Laws

His contemporaries said of Jesus, "He stirs up the people." (The same could be said of every prophet. Prophets never have the good sense to keep still about their convictions, and those who worship the status quo abhor the bad taste of those who can't, or won't, leave well enough alone, who demand change.) They were right. He did. Some of the religious leaders practically worshipped their religious laws. On the whole, Christ was obedient to the law, excepting where the law seemed a barrier to helping people. Then the welfare of persons

64

had first priority, so He healed the sick on the Sabbath, which was contrary to the ordinances of His people. He was determined not to spend His days guarding religious customs. He was slain by people who did.

Handwashing once became an issue between Him and certain scribes and Pharisees. He had matters of great importance on His mind while attending a dinner, and somehow neglected the ceremonial washing of His hands. The Pharisees questioned Him about this: "Why do your disciples not live according to the tradition of the elders, but eat with hands defiled?"

He differed with tradition concerning elaborate oath-taking, saying that a simple "Yes" or "No" was enough.

The scribes and Pharisees were known to forbid a woman to look into a mirror on the Sabbath for fear, seeing a gray hair, she might be tempted to pull it out, thus breaking the Sabbath. They debated seriously the matter of whether a good Jew could eat a hen's egg that had been laid on the Sabbath. And the Talmud prescribed which kinds of knots could be tied on the Sabbath and which knots were not allowable.

Jesus protested such trivial legalisms of that day. They placed undue emphasis upon minor matters and often neglected the weighty matters of easing human burdens, and lifting the fallen. Jesus was despised by the religious leaders, because he demanded a review of their scale of values. He was slain because He disturbed them.

Now we know He was right, and His executioners were wrong. He had established forever what counts most in the God-directed life: human helpfulness, redemptive living. Those who accept Him as Lord and Master live that way.

Trouble in Church

Remember how He caused trouble in Church? He found the exchanges of money and the sale of birds and beasts used for temple sacrifices were not being performed for the sake of the people, but for reasons of unfair profits. "In anger He overturned the tables of money-changers and the seats of those who sold pigeons," the Gospels of Matthew and Mark tell us, and Luke's Gospel adds, "He began to drive out those who sold." Mark's report is that Jesus' motivation in causing this disturbance was because the temple was intended to be "a house of prayer for all the nations," and the religious leaders had made it a place of outrageous financial gain.

A Disturbing Teacher

Saint Luke's Gospel links His teaching with attempts to assassinate him: "And he was teaching daily in the temple. The chief priests and the scribes and the principal men of the people sought to destroy him." (Luke 19:47, R.S.V.) So it has always been. He is a disturber in the Church, for what He wants most and what the Church wants are not always the same.

The Church's list of priorities may be His—but in *reverse*: bigger, more impressive buildings, more real estate, higher altars, a larger organ, softer cushions in the pews, a more renowned soprano in the choir, an inoffensive, extremely popular "name preacher" in the pulpit, and possibly a little help for the poor, the sick, the imprisoned. What the Church may place last on its list of priorities Christ puts first. That is unsettling, especially when the budget is reviewed, and some parishioner insists the scale of values does not fit the Gospel. He disturbed the Church of His day and upset Church leaders. He still would be a source of disturbance if we paid any attention to Him and made what was most important to Him most important to us.

He Upsets the State

He is a trouble-maker for the state, for what He values most the state may value least. He insists upon doing the known will of God, above all else. The state insists

upon doing the state's will, even when it conflicts with a Christ-taught conscience. His priority is an offense to our sin—sullied condition.

Jesus upsets the narrow nationalists because he insists that all people everywhere are equally precious in God's sight. Anyone who insists that presidents, congressmen and senators act in terms of the equal value of all persons is often considered an irritating nuisance or a dangerous rebel.

He Can Cause Domestic Discord

What sense do you make of the Prince of Peace saying, "Do not think that I have come to bring peace on earth; I have not come to bring peace, but a sword. For I have come to set a man against his father, and a daughter against her mother, and a daughter-in-law against her mother-in-law"? (Matthew 10:34 R.S.V.) These words come from the same lips that proclaimed, "My peace I give to you." Some war-mongers have tried to twist this teaching to mean divine support for war. But it is clear here that Christ was dealing with domestic strife, friction in the family. Matthew 12:50 shows Christ in conflict with His mother and brothers and his words quoted above may well be derived from His own family experience. When people chose Christ and made His way of life their way, it often precipitated domestic discord. It still does. Christ's views of life are in conflict with other views. What Christ and Christians value most will not agree with what others value highly.

And those who earnestly follow Him will interpret life differently than will others. All of Christ's ways will be in conflict with antichrist ways and will rub against the grain of those who futilely try to be neutral toward Him. When He comes first, as with His followers He must, other people who want to be first object. So Christ brings trouble to Christians.

His peace is found when the soul quits its feverish shifting from one loyalty to another, and its unsatisfying commitment to undeserving purposes, and comes to rest in the ultimate commitment—to Him and His way of living. The trouble He causes between persons, setting a person "at variance," comes when people make claims on us for a loyalty that must be reserved for God alone. When people ask us to lie for them, cheat for them, side with them against our better judgment, or in anyway compromise our standards for their sakes, Christ causes trouble, for he demands absolute faithfulness to the Christ-taught conscience.

Shame and Salvation

Simon Peter, one of the founders of the Church, looked at Jesus and was ashamed of what he was and how he behaved. He exclaimed, "Depart from me, for I am a sinful man, O Lord" (Luke 5:8). Until Peter met Jesus he probably felt passably good and may have used our own self-defensive phrase, "I'm as good as the next fellow." But beside the towering goodness of Jesus, Peter felt small and unworthy.

Of course, Jesus did not heed Peter's bidding. He did not depart. He stayed. And out of that self-consciousness and shame of Simon Peter emerged Peter, the Apostle. Peter's troubled humiliation was the beginning of radical change. The hidden possibilities that developed under Christ's mastery until the unstable Simon became Peter, "the rock," were realized only after this disciple became ashamed of himself.

Until He troubles us, Christ cannot save us. Such trouble is the beginning of redemption.

The only chance civilization has for survival is if enough people get profoundly disturbed about injustices heaped upon minority races, minority religions and upon the poor; economic exploitation of the masses through deceitful advertising and hidden taxes; the war-method of solving international conflicts; a decline in moral standards as shown by a rise in illegitimate births, rising divorce rates, rising crime rates, increased use of drugs; pollution of our natural environment, and a multitude of other evils. Only if we are profoundly troubled, and ashamed of our part in world evils, will we do anything about the world's wrongs, just as some people will only visit a doctor if their pain becomes unbearable.

One of Martin Luther's teachers in the Augustinian monastery at Erfurt, Germany advised him, "Brother Martin, let the Bible alone: read the old teachers. They give you the whole marrow of the Bible. Reading the Bible simply breeds unrest."

Sitting at the feet of Christ, listening to Him, pondering what He means and our relationship to Him, breeds unrest, too. But it is an unrest and dissatisfaction with self that saves.

Christ Shows Us
Our True Worth

A person has hardly visited a rocky lake shore at all until he has walked there in the company of a geologist who knows and loves stones. The geologist sees what the person unlearned in geology never notices. Picking up a rough, dull-appearing, commonplace stone from the beach, the geologist wipes it off on his trousers, takes a harder stone and knocks off a bit of the first rock, then holds that rough particle of the earth's crust up to the sun to be blessed by its light.

He shows his companion a touch of feldspar on one side of the rock, a splendid sparkle of quartz on the other side, and all over the surface bright flashes of mica. Before the wondering eyes of the novice the expert, by his knowledge, insight, and appreciation, transforms a common stone into a rare gem. In his hands the ordinary rock suddenly becomes a treasure.

Thus in the company of Christ we are saved from our dull perception of the world, of our birth, our daily life, our vocation, our marriage, our destiny. Through Him all things become more meaningful. Especially He saves us from our dim, drab, jaded awareness of values in human nature, and reveals all persons, including ourselves, as having infinite worth in God's sight.

The Worst and the Best

Saint John's Gospel makes the claim that Jesus "knew what was in man." He knew that man can be terribly indifferent to the beauty of God's world, to God's truth, love and goodness. He knew the depths of man's depravity, his perverted instincts and desires, his meanness and cruelty. And He saw the worst not only in his enemies, but touches of it in His best friend.

But Christ also knew, better than any other person who ever lived, the possibilities for good in the life controlled by a consciousness of God. He knew the rankling dissatisfaction of men with what they were, their terrible consciousness of guilt, their craving to be better and their helplessness to be what they ought by their own powers alone. He knew the best and worst about men. And knowing all about men, He loved them.

Broken for You

As Christ drew nearer the cross, on the very night before His crucifixion, what did He say about human worth? Remember it? At the Last Supper with His

73

disciples he took bread and broke it and said, "This is my body which is broken for *you*." This was the value He placed on human nature. He would willingly die for the sake of people like ourselves. He was not speaking to perfected saints. Most of them who heard Him would, within a few hours, desert Him in His time of greatest need. Even Simon Peter would abandon Him. Nevertheless, for that sort of sin-ridden person Christ would lay down His life.

Atonement Theories

How Christ's death long ago can help us in our own day has always mystified men. How can a tragedy on Golgotha help us? All kinds of theories have been advanced to explain this, some of them bizarre, almost insane, and others that make good sense, or, better yet, glad Gospel. The "ransom theory" holds that man was the captive of Satan, kidnapped away from God. Christ was the ransom God paid Satan to get man back.

The "penal satisfaction theory" argues that man deserved punishment for his sin as surely as a criminal deserves jail. Man must pay for his crime. So, to satisfy God, man had to be punished for his sin. But Christ volunteered to endure an amount of suffering equivalent to what the entire human race deserved, thus satisfying God's sense of justice.

The "commercial theory," advanced by Anselm in 1033, says that by sinning man robbed God of His honor. Man owed obedience to God but could not pay.

Jesus laid down His life on the cross as His free gift to God to pay man's awful debt. This view makes it appear that the crucifixion is but a commercial transaction, a piece of moral bargaining in some swap shop.

Horace Bushnell and others developed a "moral influence theory," propounding that Christ's atoning death has a strong effect upon man because it brings heavy moral force to bear upon us, revealing God's love, thereby softening our hearts and leading us to repentence.

All such theories are at best partial and incomplete. Some are so intellectually awkward and devoid of high moral content that they offend us. But when they are all reduced to their essence, what they attempt to say is plain, good and begins and ends with great, glad news: God loves you. You count with God. But you cannot be what you ought to be by effort alone. Try as you may, effort alone leaves you far short of perfection. You still sin, if not in gross, outrageous ways, then in small and obscure ways. But you sin. However, God loves you and longs to reclaim you.

"You sin" can truthfully be said about the finest person we know. At the cross we see Christ killed not by the worst men, but by the best, by religious leaders, men who considered themselves dedicated servants of the Most High, and by Romans who stood for law and order. God's Best and Perfect One was slain by the best people of His day, showing us that our very best can be very ugly and is never good enough to suit God. Therefore we all need forgiveness. Through the cross

75

of Christ we see Love going all the way to make God's forgiveness dramatically real to us.

Christ's sacrificial death unites our need with God's love, our helplessness with God's help, our failure, humiliation, spiritual poverty, our pain, sorrow, loneliness and our despair, to God's victory over all that is anti-God.

It Works

Fortunately, our continued bafflement about how Christ's death helps us does not weaken the effect of the cross. In spite of mysteries surrounding that sacrificial death, it still saves us.

It is claimed that according to the theory of aerodynamics a honeybee cannot fly. An airplane-like body, modeled after the body of a honeybee, can be placed in a wind-tunnel, where airships are factory-tested, and it can thereby be proven beyond the shadow of a doubt that a honeybee cannot fly. The shape, size and weight of the bee in relation to the total wingspread make flying impossible. But the bee, ignorant of model-making, wind-tunnels, factory-testing, engineering and scientific formulas goes ahead, anyway, with its nectar collecting business, flying all over the sweet-scented landscape.

So, although full understanding of the meaning of Christ's death will always elude us, since the day that central event of history millions of people around this cross-shadowed globe have sung, "He died for me."

The thought of the cross of Christ is, for Christians,

food and drink for the mind and nourishment for the soul. It is a revelation of something about man, his worth in Christ's sight, and therefore in God's sight. And it is a revelation of the most vital truth about God: God loves us not only for what we might be, but just as we are. "This is my body broken for you," was spoken to sinful men.

This truth is the heart and soul of Christianity. Cut it out and Christianity is nothing but a dead shell. Keep that truth central, man's worth to a loving God, and the Church will live healthily, devoting itself to the worship of God and to sacrificial helpfulness toward all earth's children, whom God loves and for whom Christ died.